Streets of Edinburgh

Gavin Booth

Ian Allan
60th
ANNIVERSARY

Introduction

Even allowing for my natural bias, it is surely fair to say that Edinburgh is one of the world's most attractive cities. After more than half a century as a resident I am still amazed and delighted by the constantly changing vistas it presents.

Princes Street is now very much the focal point of the city, and, although it has been allowed to become an architectural mess and most of the shops are replicated on every UK high street, it has that breathtaking backdrop of the Castle and the Old Town, and beyond that the dramatic bulk of Arthur's Seat, Edinburgh's own mini-mountain, dominating the landscape from all directions.

The New Town, built in the 18th century, was well established when proper public transport developed in Victorian times, first horsebuses then horse trams. But Edinburgh, almost uniquely in the UK, went from horse-drawn to cable-driven trams, prompted no doubt by the city's many hills. Neighbouring Leith and Musselburgh sensibly opted for electric trams, and, following Leith's merger into Edinburgh in 1920, the city finally decided to scrap its outdated and temperamental cable cars and go for electric cars. The last cable cars ran in 1923, but few mourned them. Some had their lives prolonged as electric cars, but one consequence of Edinburgh's late conversion was that it built up a modern fleet of trams, most dating from the 1920s and 1930s. Other cities were stuck with trams built in the early years of the 20th century, which often hastened the demise of these systems.

Motorbuses really took off in Edinburgh through the efforts of the Scottish Motor Traction (SMT) company, which from 1906 pioneered routes into the Lothians, beyond the reach of the city trams. SMT became the parent company for a group that eventually covered most of Scotland, and in postwar years became the Scottish Bus Group. SMT's influence spread throughout southeast Scotland, with service networks in the Borders and long-distance routes to London and other parts of England. But its roots remained firmly in Edinburgh.

Edinburgh Corporation moved tentatively into motorbuses after World War 1, using them to serve areas where there was no tramway — notably the Easter Road–Holyrood–High Street–Fountainbridge corridor — and increasingly to serve the public housing that was being built on what were then the fringes of the city.

This book covers the 30 years following the end of World War 2, though the lack of suitable colour photographs has meant that the earliest date from the 1950s. They show a city that has changed less than its old rival, Glasgow, 40-odd miles to the west, partly because of a strong lobby to protect Edinburgh's architectural heritage.

At the end of the war the Edinburgh tramway network had reached its peak. Extensions planned in the 1930s were abandoned, but still new trams were being turned out at the

Previous page: The Scott Monument provides an excellent vantage point for visitors to understand the topography of Edinburgh. Looking along Princes Street towards the east end, there are surprisingly few buses around for 1.20pm on a Wednesday afternoon in July 1964. The smoke-blackened mass of the North British Hotel still dominates the view, though it has since been cleaned and renamed The Balmoral. To the right of the hotel is Waverley station, which 'the NB' hotel was built in 1902 to serve. The globe-topped tower sits atop what was R. W. Forsyth's store, and slightly to its right is the dome of Robert Adam's elegant Register House. The row of shop blinds marks the city's main Woolworth's store, today a variety of different high-street shops. Beyond the NB clock is Calton Hill, dominated by the unfinished National Monument, intended to be a replica of the Parthenon. Above the central part of the NB rises St Andrew's House, built in the late 1930s as Scotland's government offices. Surprisingly, just two buses are visible in this view — an Edinburgh Corporation Leyland Titan turning on to the North Bridge, and a No 26 heading down Waterloo Place towards Princes Street. *Iain MacGregor*

First published 2002

ISBN 0 7110 2866 4

© Ian Allan Publishing Ltd 2002

Published by Ian Allan Publishing

an imprint of Ian Allan Publishing Ltd, Hersham, Surrey KT12 4RG.
Printed by Ian Allan Printing Ltd, Hersham, Surrey KT12 4RG.

Code: 0207/B2

Corporation's Shrubhill Works; 18 new domed-roof standards appeared between 1945 and 1950. But fashion was turning against the tram, and a new Transport Manager, Moris Little, pushed through a programme of complete replacement by motorbuses in the 1950s. The last Edinburgh tram ran in November 1956, and there was massive investment in new and rebuilt buses.

In the meantime the SMT group had sold out into state ownership, and although the buses continued to show SMT as their fleetname, the company was now strictly Scottish Omnibuses Ltd (SOL). A new bus station was built by SOL for its own and associated companies' services, and this was opened in April 1957. Before this time the buses had used the centre of St Andrew Square as a city terminus. The bus station was built over in the early 1970s and continued to function until July 2000, when it was closed to make way for a major retail development,

which incorporates a covered coach station. From the mid-1960s SOL adopted the fleetname 'EASTERN SCOTTISH', later reverting to 'SMT', and the company is now part of First Edinburgh.

Edinburgh Corporation ceased to exist at the time of Scottish regionalisation in May 1975; Lothian Region took over the Corporation's transport responsibilities, and that year provides a sensible cut-off point for this book.

The photographs in this book have been gathered from a number of sources, individually acknowledged after each caption. If a disproportionate number show scenes in Princes Street, that is because so much of the city's life revolves around this

Looking west along Princes Street from the Scott Monument reveals more buses but comparatively little traffic overall — certainly not enough to warrant much traffic control at The Mound / Hanover Street junction in the centre of the photograph, which looks like a free-for-all but was normally overseen by a points policeman. Daimler and Leyland Corporation buses negotiate the traffic, and a Scottish Omnibuses AEC Regal IV coach, one of a fleet bought for Edinburgh–London overnight services in 1951, is the cream vehicle nearest to the camera. Below the camera is part of East Princes Street Gardens, and beyond the Royal Scottish Academy — in the midst of its stone-cleaning in this September 1961 view — West Princes Street Gardens stretch towards the red sandstone bulk of the Caledonian Hotel, the city's other big railway hotel, completed in 1903. The main spires on the left horizon belong to Sir George Gilbert Scott's Gothic masterpiece for the Episcopal church, St Mary's Cathedral. The mix of architectural styles that characterises Princes Street today was already evident, but Victorian piles like the North British & Mercantile Insurance building that dominates the centre right of the photograph would shortly be demolished for the British Home Stores development, and the dark stone buildings beside the three eastbound buses, which housed the Life Association of Scotland offices and the New Club, would also fall under the demolition hammer. *Iain MacGregor*

thoroughfare, and a substantial proportion of the city's tram and bus routes use it. Many will remember the apparently endless lines of stately trams that seemed to be an integral part of the streetscape for so many years; in 1938, for example, most of the dozen tram routes that served the whole of the street maintained at least a 10-minute frequency all day, right to the last trams at around 11.30pm, and between mid-afternoon and early evening frequencies on the core routes were increased to give a total of some 100 trams an hour in each direction — and that's not counting the extra cars that were regularly slipped into the system. Today there is a high level of bus provision, possibly more noticeable on the north (shops) side, where traffic other than buses and taxis is banned. The south side is set to follow. Even today, Lothian Buses runs 30 all-day services along Princes Street, offering a combined frequency of two a minute in each direction.

Edinburgh has always enjoyed high-quality public transport, and for the past 40 years this has largely been street-based. The city's once-significant local rail network was seriously eroded in the 1960s, and only a handful of suburban stations survived the Beeching axe. Now that is changing, with new stations and exciting plans for more local services. Not only that but it looks as if Edinburgh will see trams again in the next decade, linking the city centre with important new residential and commercial developments at Granton, on the Firth of Forth, and on the city's western extremities.

Two operators dominate the city's street transport today — Lothian Buses, successor to Edinburgh Corporation, and First Edinburgh, successor to SMT. Service frequencies are high, fares are relatively low, and there is continued investment in state-of-the-art buses. None of this would have been possible without the pioneering efforts of their predecessors, who enjoyed their highest passenger loadings ever in those years following World War 2 when car ownership was still for the privileged few and television was yet to reach Scotland. Just look at these photos and marvel at the empty streets — and recall the days when you could legally park your car on Princes Street all day.

While the 1950s represented the start of a slow decline for bus operators all over Britain, the city's commitment to public transport over many years has helped to arrest this and means that Edinburgh can still boast one of the best bus systems in the country.

My thanks are due to the photographers and agencies who responded to my call for photographs — Campbell Sayers, Colour-Rail, C. Carter, Iain MacGregor and Photobus. Many of the fine tram photographs supplied by Colour-Rail are available from that organisation at 5 Treacher's Close, Chesham HP5 2HD, quoting the reference numbers (where shown) in the appropriate captions. Photobus also sells prints and slides showing trams and buses in Edinburgh.

The photographs are arranged in broadly geographic groups, starting inevitably with Princes Street (where most transport photographers still seem to congregate) and then moving out from the centre to the suburbs. They portray a public transport system that has done much for the economy of this fine city. If you remember this period, wallow in the nostalgia. If you don't, marvel at how much some things have changed — and how some things seem not to have changed at all.

Gavin Booth
Edinburgh
April 2002

A 1961 view that clearly illustrates the division between Edinburgh's Old and New towns, taken from the Castle, itself firmly dominating the Old Town. Building of the New Town was started in the 18th century to the north, to relieve overcrowding and insanitary conditions on the ridge stretching from the Castle to Holyrood. What had been the Nor' Loch was drained and now houses Princes Street Gardens and the railway lines from the north and west, tunnelling under William Playfair's 1845 National Gallery to the sprawl of Waverley station, centre right in the photograph. An Edinburgh Corporation Leyland Titan descends The Mound from the south towards Princes Street while another picks up passengers outside the Royal Scottish Academy, again by Playfair, which fronts on to Princes Street. Waverley Bridge crosses the station, and beyond it the North Bridge crosses the railway at a higher level. Behind is the Calton Hill, dominated in this view by the Nelson Monument, in the shape of an up-ended telescope. In the centre of the photograph, looking as if it is set for take-off, is the Scott Monument, completed in 1844 as a memorial to the Scottish novelist, Sir Walter Scott. In the left distance, above the buildings of the New Town, lies Leith, the city's port, sitting on the Firth of Forth, which separates Edinburgh from the Kingdom of Fife. *Iain MacGregor*

A 1967 Corporation Leyland Atlantean turns from the North Bridge on to Princes Street at its east end. On the right can be seen the Nelson Monument on Calton Hill and one of the twin porticos framing Waterloo Place, built following Wellington's victory in 1815. The building on the left is Robert Adam's 18th-century Register House, and in front of it, facing towards the North Bridge, is John Steell's heroic statue of the Duke of Wellington — known locally as the Iron Duke, in bronze, by Steell! The buildings behind the front of the bus mark the top end of Leith Street, falling sharply away towards Leith Walk. *Campbell Sayers*

A newly delivered Corporation Leyland Titan PD2 with Falkirk-built Alexander body at the east end of Princes Street in March 1962. It has just picked up passengers outside the North British Hotel and is passing the Waverley Market, then the city's exhibition hall but now the site of a large indoor shopping centre. Calton Hill, with the National and Nelson's monuments, can be seen on the horizon, and, while the buildings on the left of the picture are still largely unchanged, none of the retailers survives in this block; Forsyth of Edinburgh (not to be confused with R. W. Forsyth on the facing corner), H. Samuel, Etam and John Collier have given way to other retailers, two of them selling mobile phones. The late-19th-century Royal British Hotel still welcomes visitors to the city. The fact that control of the junction was left to a white-coated policeman on points duty in the midst of the traffic fumes is a reminder of less environmentally conscious times. The bus is on the 3 route to Saughton Mains through the busy streets of Gorgie, a service that replaced the 3 tram in 1953 — one of the earliest tram withdrawals.
Iain MacGregor

Above: There are very few good colour photographs of Edinburgh tramcars in the days before 1952, when commercial advertising started to appear on the side panels. This June 1951 view shows tram No 48, one of the last standard cars built by the Corporation at Shrubhill between 1934 and 1950. The driver of this 10 tram to Bernard Street, Leith, is chatting to the pointsman at the South St Andrew Street junction. Behind the tram is R. W. Forsyth's store, and on the left is the C. & A. Modes store that would be destroyed in a dramatic fire in 1955. *C. Carter*

Right: Passengers boarding the Princes Street trams used islands placed at regular intervals along the street. Here a standard car, built by R. Y. Pickering at Wishaw, collects passengers at the loading island adjacent to the Scott Monument in July 1955. The buildings visible are, from the left, the famous Jenners department store (complete with Royal Warrant crest), the tall 1883 Old Waverley Hotel and the original C&A store. Pickering built 10 of these trams to the standard Edinburgh Corporation design in 1932, the first cars built other than at ECT's Shrubhill Works since 1924. No 257 would be withdrawn in October 1955, as would the No 9 tram, which linked Granton, on the Forth foreshore, through the city centre to the pleasant western suburb of Colinton. *T. J. Edgington / Colour-Rail (IR162)*

Left: At the same spot, on the same day in July 1955, the photographer gives us a close-up view of one of Edinburgh's 'streamliners', the 23 trams bought in 1934/5 from three different builders. No 262, heading for Granton on the 10, was one of three built in 1934 by English Electric, while No 28, appropriately on the 28 to Stanley Road, is one of six built in 1935 by Metro-Cammell, whose product could be distinguished from the others by the position of its route number. The bus on the tram-replacement 3 service is one of 60 wartime Guy Arabs bought from London Transport, rebuilt by the corporation and rebodied by Duple in 1952/3. *T. J. Edgington / Colour-Rail (IR163)*

Above: Every bus-company chief engineer's nightmare — a disabled bus being towed along the main street in the middle of the day. In June 1975 this Eastern Scottish AEC Matador was photographed hauling an engineless Daimler Fleetline with Eastern Coach Works body along Princes Street. British Home Stores now occupies the site of the former North British & Mercantile building, and the other buildings behind the bus, including more shops and a hotel, vividly demonstrate the architectural hotchpotch that is Princes Street. *Gavin Booth*

Left: Festival Edinburgh in August 1974, with a year-old Corporation Leyland Atlantean drawing in to the first bus stop west of The Mound. The background has changed little in the past quarter of a century; the city's planners and amenity groups rather belatedly realised what was happening to the street and ensured that new developments have been rather more sympathetic to the townscape. The bus is heading for Wester Hailes, the substantial late-1960s / early-1970s public housing development on the western fringes of the city; buses served the area even as it was being built, and the Wester Hailes Centre is now an important bus interchange. *Gavin Booth*

Above left: A fine September 1955 view looking west along Princes Street with Corporation tram No 260, built in 1933 by Metropolitan-Cammell near Birmingham. This flat-topped body design had first appeared the previous year on a tram built by ECT at Shrubhill, and contributed towards the development of the standard car of the mid-1930s. It is bound for Stanley Road, more strictly Newhaven, on the Firth of Forth. Also visible are various ECT tram-replacement buses and a rebodied SOL AEC Regal double-decker. Just visible above the Marcus furs shop are the three stuffed bears that will be remembered by many citizens and visitors. Although the city's tramway system still has 14 months more life, there are surprisingly few cars in evidence on this summer morning. *C. Banks collection / Colour-Rail*

Above: The bears had gone from the Marcus shop by February 1974, as still-gleaming brand-new Leyland Atlantean AN68 No 921 heads westwards along Princes Street. The eastbound carriageway is busy with a mix of traffic; today only buses and taxis may use this side of Princes Street. No 921 is heading for Juniper Green, on the city's western boundary. The symbols on either side of the destination display show that the bus is fitted with the Autofare ticket system, where passengers dropped their fares into the red hopper visible beside the driver. No change was given on these driver-only buses. *Gavin Booth*

Left: Ambassador Coaches bloomed briefly in the 1970s as a local coach company with an interesting taste in new vehicles. Here a rare Portuguese-built AEC-UTIC coach heads west along Princes Street in March 1974, followed by another coach from the same fleet. The grey buildings above the coach replaced the Victorian New Club and Life Association buildings in the late 1960s. *Gavin Booth*

Below: Carrying 'tram boards' (a term still in use today) advertising connections with the Ideal Home Exhibition, Leyland Titan No 768 is heading west on Princes Street in May 1970 on the long 11 service linking Newhaven in the north with Fairmilehead, to the southwest of the city. Edinburgh always favoured long cross-city routes, avoiding the need for city-centre termini and offering a wider variety of links. A Morris van used by the city department store J. & R. Allan passes, and above the van can be seen the first-floor balconies which the Princes Street Panel, set up in 1954, required as part of a misguided plan to provide end-to-end walkways along the whole street. The idea was later dropped, but there are still isolated stretches of balcony along the street.
Arnold Richardson / Photobus

This excellent high-level view taken from a building just west of the South Charlotte Street intersection shows four domed-roof standard cars and a selection of Corporation Daimler and Leyland buses. Taken late in the afternoon in high summer — the only time the sun is high enough to offer this opportunity — it shows the trams in 1956 in their final months. Nearest the camera, No 226 is bound for Braids and No 230 for Granton. All four trams are from the 84 domed-roof standards built by the Corporation at Shrubhill between 1934 and 1950. The red-roofed buildings in the top right, above West Princes Street Gardens, are in Ramsay Garden — a very desirable city address — and the twin towers to their left belong to the University's New College. The Church of Scotland's Assembly Hall is within this complex, and provided the first, temporary home for Scotland's Parliament. The dark domed building to the left of the Assembly Hall is the head office of the Bank of Scotland — now stone-cleaned, like so many of the city's public buildings.
J. Copland / Photobus

In the days when you could park your car in Princes Street without any difficulty and without any fear of fines or removal, three Shrubhill standards glide along the tramway one morning in September 1955 amid a handful of cars and shoppers. Darling & Company was a ladies' outfitters, and west of this store is Moffat, the photographers, and travel agents Thos Cook. Between the two trams is the built-out frontage of the Monseigneur News Theatre, offering a continuous programme of cartoons and newsreels in those days before television became more widespread.

C. Banks collection / Colour-Rail

Tram No 237 heads east along Princes Street in 1955 on the famous No 6 Marchmont Circle service that linked Princes Street, the Bridges, Marchmont, Tollcross and Lothian Road in both directions.

This domed-roof standard was built at Shrubhill in 1936 and survived until 1956. The barriers and bunting suggest a Royal visit was imminent. *T. Marsh / Colour-Rail*

In the period covered by this book, all of Scottish Omnibuses' sister companies in the Scottish Bus Group operated longer-distance services into Edinburgh, but Lanarkshire-based Central SMT was probably the least familiar. This 1961 Central Leyland Leopard L1 with Alexander body is turning from Castle Street on to Princes Street on the infrequent service to Lanark via Midcalder in March 1969. The buildings in the background survive relatively unchanged, except that the premises then occupied by the National Commercial Bank and Green's hairdressers are now a Burger King fast-food outlet. Castle Street is now closed off at its Princes Street junction. *Iain MacGregor*

Left: Few if any passengers are aboard this 1947 SOL AEC Regal in Princes Street heading for Ratho, a canalside village to the west of Edinburgh. Still carrying the SMT diamond fleetname and the attractive light green and cream colours, it is about to pass, on the extreme left of the picture, the News Theatre, at various times the Monseigneur and the Jacey. Next door is W. Jamieson & Sons, one of the privately owned shops that once characterised Princes Street. The Royal crest is a reminder of the many local suppliers which provided goods for HM The Queen when she was in residence at the Palace of Holyroodhouse. *J. T. Inglis*

Below: Heading for Shandwick Place — always a busy corridor, with most westbound tram and then bus routes filtered through it — Corporation Atlantean No 871 on the 33 heads for Wester Hailes while a red Mini turns left into Lothian Road, in May 1970. The dominant building on the left of the bus was built last century for McVities, Guest, the well-known Edinburgh bakery and tea-room. *Arnold Richardson / Photobus*

Above: On a dull July day in 1959 an unpainted Corporation Leyland Titan PD2 brightens the scene in Shandwick Place, the western continuation of Princes Street. Unpainted buses were briefly fashionable in the 1950s and early 1960s, and in 1957 the Corporation bought 10 to add to one purchased in 1955. All 11 were painted normally in madder and white during 1959. No 795 is on the 26 service to the spacious 1950s hilltop housing scheme at Clermiston; note the Zoo Park 'tram board'. The Roman Baroque church, St George's West, dominates Victorian Shandwick Place. *Gavin Booth collection*

Right: Looking from Princes Street down Waverley Bridge, you can't ignore the dramatic backdrop of grey stone houses rising up on the edges of the Castle rock. In the 16th and 17th centuries Edinburgh built some of the earliest multi-storey housing in the world, and, while a few examples survive, most of the buildings in this photograph date from later periods. Austin FX4 taxis sit waiting their turn to roll down the carriageway into Waverley station as Corporation Leyland Tiger Cub / Weymann No 80 sets off on the short service 60 towards Holyrood in January 1974. *Gavin Booth*

Left: A Sunday-morning closure of the North Bridge has brought extra traffic on to Waverley Bridge, literally on top of Waverley station, in March 1974. As traffic queues back from the junction with Princes Street, dominated by the bulk of the 1950s C&A store, an Edinburgh Corporation 1970 Leyland Atlantean with Alexander bodywork heads south for Marchmont past a knot of ECT inspectors overseeing the smooth running of the bus services. A black-and-white-painted Bedford coach sits at the top of the bridge, ready to depart for the airport. *Gavin Booth*

Above: For long the departure point for the Corporation's City Tours programme, Waverley Bridge is now considerably busier, with the buses of three competing open-top tour operations, plus the high-frequency Airlink service to the airport. In October 1969 two Bedford SB coaches with Duple bodies, dating from 1963/4, sit waiting for passengers. They are in the black-and-white livery adopted for the Corporation's coach fleet in the 1950s. In the background, an Eastern Scottish Bristol Lodekka turns on to Waverley Bridge, having fought its way from New Street depot through the fruit markets of Market Street. The grey mass of Old Town buildings is topped by the crown tower of the High Kirk of St Giles, in the High Street. *Roy Marshall / Photobus*

Left: Sitting outside the tourist information office at the top of the Waverley Bridge in June 1970, which doubled as the departure point for the service to Edinburgh Airport at Turnhouse, is Corporation No 101, a famous bus. A Leyland Leopard with Alexander body, it was new in 1961 as a three-door Continental-style bus, but was not successful in this guise and became a more conventional single-door bus for the airport service in 1969. It is now preserved, splendidly restored to its 1961 condition. It remained unique in the UK.
The tourist office was in part of the old Waverley Market exhibition hall, since demolished to make way for the Princes Mall shopping centre. *Roy Marshall / Photobus*

Above: Crossing Princes Street from Hanover Street towards The Mound in August 1955, tram 204 is on the 23 route for Morningside station — always one of the city's busiest and most profitable routes. Diners in the Brown Derby restaurant behind the tram enjoy their first-floor view of the cityscape. The tram is flying coloured pennants from its trolley rope, as was normal for special occasions such as Royal visits and the annual Festival. Tram 204 was one of an amazing total of 26 of these standards built by the Corporation at its Shrubhill Works off Leith Walk in 1935; this was the first year of production of these cars, when up to three a month were produced. *J. T. Inglis / Colour-Rail*

Below: The tram tracks at the foot of The Mound, where it meets Princes Street, curve to the left in the path of tram No 103 and then sweep to the right to allow trams to turn comfortably left into Hanover Street. Tram 103, Shrubhill-built in 1935, is caught in the late-afternoon summer sunshine, heading north to Granton Road station. The pillars on the right belong to the Royal Scottish Academy. *Colour-Rail*

Right: Nearly 20 years after the last trams, and the 23 and 27 bus routes still use The Mound, their routes still very clearly based on the tram routes that carried the same route numbers. The Royal Scottish Academy has been stone-cleaned in the meantime, and Edinburgh Corporation has moved on to longer buses, in this case a 1964 Leyland Titan PD3 with forward-entrance Alexander body. The February 1974 sunshine shows the stone-cleaned RSA to good effect. *Gavin Booth*

Left: With the towers of New College and the Highland Tolbooth church rising behind, tram No 69 climbs The Mound towards the Old Town on the 27 service to suburban Craiglockhart on a fine evening in July 1955. No 69 was important in the Edinburgh tram story; it was the 1934 prototype for the 84 standards that were built at Shrubhill over the next 16 years. Similar car No 35 has been preserved. The conductor, on the rear platform, is wearing a white top to his cap, as all Corporation platform staff did between 1 May and 30 September each year. *C. Banks collection / Colour-Rail (IR230)*

Above: The young ladies in July 1955 appear to be unnaturally interested in 25-year-old Shrubhill wooden standard car No 198 carefully making its way round the sharp curves on The Mound with New College in the background. The silver-and-black steel post in the foreground was one of several installed in 1924 to deal with derailed trams, though it is difficult to see how they could prevent a tram dropping on to the railway lines below. *C. Banks collection / Colour-Rail (IR232)*

Above: Full-frontal 1956 view of 1935-built Shrubhill standard No 83 descending The Mound towards Princes Street on route 23. Note the distinctive silver-painted lamp-posts, once a feature of the city centre. The monument in the background is the Black Watch South African war memorial. No 83 was one of the trams that took part in the sad procession on the last night of the city's trams on Friday 16 November 1956. *J. Copland / Photobus*

Right: Bus No 42 on the 42 route climbs The Mound towards the Old Town in July 1975, by which time the city's bus fleet was in the ownership of Lothian Region Transport. It is a 1973 Leyland Atlantean AN68 with Alexander body, and rising majestically above it is the dramatic bulk of Edinburgh Castle and, on the left, the houses of Ramsay Garden. The 1924 tram posts are still in evidence — and indeed are still there today. *Gavin Booth*

Left: Until 1957 the bus services of SMT and later Scottish Omnibuses used the centre of St Andrew Square as their main city-centre terminal point. In June 1951 the driver of a 1938 Leyland Titan TD5, No J52, changes the destination blind before departure. Behind is a 1949 AEC Regent III with Duple bodywork — one of the first new buses to be delivered in the green livery that Scottish Omnibuses adopted in 1949 to replace the blue worn by SMT buses since 1930 and still carried by the Leyland at this stage. The tramlines in the foreground are a reminder that trams and other traffic circumnavigated the square, but the trams had gone by the time the buses were moved off the street into the brand-new bus station in 1957. *C. Carter*

Below left: St Andrew Square bus station was opened by Scottish Omnibuses in April 1957 on city-centre land that the company had acquired gradually over a number of years. As originally built, the main bus station consisted of four platforms for local services and an area for tours and express services. The city fathers insisted that a stone portico should be provided at the point where buses exited on to the square itself, to preserve the amenity of the area. Leaving the bus station in September 1958 is a Guy Arab with Weymann utility bodywork delivered to SMT just after the end of World War 2, in August 1945. The rather basic body is to the lowbridge layout used by SOL and many other fleets at the time, with a side gangway upstairs and awkward four-across seating. This layout was rendered obsolete by the Bristol Lodekka, as seen in the background, which allowed normal seating on both decks within the 'lowbridge' height of roughly 13ft 6in. The Guy is heading for South Queensferry, in the shadow of the Forth Railway Bridge. *Gavin Booth collection*

Pulling on to St Andrew Square in 1964 is a Scottish Omnibuses AEC Reliance with Park Royal bodywork, which had been new in 1959, heading west for the historic town of Linlithgow. It carries the short-lived 'Scottish' fleetname that would shortly be replaced by 'EASTERN SCOTTISH', and the bright green colour would give way to a darker shade. This area has changed greatly in the intervening 40 years; even the then-new office block on the left of the photograph has been replaced. *Campbell Sayers*

Above: The cramped nature of the bus station is captured in this June 1963 view showing a 1946 AEC Regal with Duple bodywork, surrounded by other SOL buses as it makes ready to set out for Bo'ness. Most of the tenements in the background were demolished in the late 1960s to make way for the St James Centre development of offices and shops. *A. J. Douglas / Photobus*

Right: In 1970 the bus station was built over, further limiting the space for passengers and buses, and buses now emerged into St Andrew Square from under an office block. A stranger on the 16 route in March 1973 is this Bristol Lodekka FLF6G with Eastern Coach Works body in the colours of the Norwich-based Eastern Counties company. Eastern Scottish had bought 35 rear-engined Bristol VRTs in 1968/9, but hadn't liked them and swapped them with Lodekkas like this one from National Bus Company fleets in England. The Travellers' Tryst bar on the left was also owned by Scottish Omnibuses. *Gavin Booth*

TRAVELLERS TRYST LOUNGE BAR

16

EASTERN COUNTIES

ONG 349F

Below: Bus companies were hard-pressed to get new vehicles in the early postwar years, and Edinburgh Corporation managed to stake a claim for 72 buses that were built largely to the unique specification of Birmingham City Transport. The 'Birmingham Daimlers' were received in 1949/50, and some survived right to 1967. In St Andrew Square in 1964 is No 179 on the 11 route to Fairmilehead. Behind and alongside the bus are the two symmetrical pavilions designed by Robert Adam in 1769 to flank the Royal Bank of Scotland (not visible here, as it is set back from the square), which had been built as a house for Sir Laurence Dundas. *Campbell Sayers*

Right: Following the opening of the Forth Road Bridge in September 1964, regular direct bus services were provided for the first time between Edinburgh and towns in Fife and beyond. Passing through St Andrew Square in June 1970 against a backdrop of 18th- and 19th-century offices on the north side of the square is a 1966 Alexander (Fife) AEC Reliance with Alexander Y-type body, which has just left the bus station on its way to Perth. Parking meters and unusually empty spaces circle the gardens in the centre of the square, where Scottish Omnibuses services had terminated until the bus station opened in 1957. *Iain MacGregor*

Below: George Street was the axis of the original New Town, built from 1767, and lies along a natural ridge parallel with Princes Street to the south. It has never enjoyed the same level of tram or bus services as Princes Street, and has tended to house prestigious banks and offices, as well as rather more upmarket shops; today many of the banks have become bars and restaurants. At the east end of George Street in June 1973 is Corporation No 998, a bus that remained unique in the fleet. It was the first 30ft-long Leyland Titan PD3 for the undertaking, bought in 1957, and boasted this glassfibre Homalloy front on its Alexander body. It is on the 19 Circle, its normal home, sitting outside the impressive 18th-century Parish Church of St Andrew & St George. The building with the flagpoles is the 19th-century George Hotel. *Roy Marshall / Photobus*

Right: Turning from the west end of George Street on to Charlotte Square in 1964 is a 1956 Guy Arab IV with Alexander bodywork. The buildings in the background have not changed greatly — although their occupants have, possibly several times over — and there has been a laudable move at this end of the street to remove some added-on shops and restore the frontages to their original Georgian splendour. Some ill-conceived 1960s buildings have disappeared completely, and new 'Georgian' buildings have been erected in their place. Only the crisp cleanliness of the stonework gives the game away. *Campbell Sayers*

Above: Charlotte Square, at the west end of George Street and balancing St Andrew Square, is widely recognised as the icing on the New Town cake, and the north side is universally admired. Designed by Robert Adam and built in the 18th century, the centrepiece of the terrace (immediately beside the coach) is Bute House, now the official residence of Scotland's First Minister. A Southdown Leyland Leopard coach with Plaxton body, in National white, pauses in the square on an extended tour in July 1975. The barriers are for yet another Royal visit. *Gavin Booth*

Right: Passengers pile aboard tram No 218, bound for Fairmilehead on the 11 service, outside the Caledonian Hotel in Lothian Road in July 1955. The loading islands were surprisingly narrow, and this one has the portcullis-style tram-stop plate introduced in the later tramway years. The Caledonian, one of the city's five-star hotels, was built by the eponymous railway company in 1902. No 218 was built by ECT at Shrubhill; it was new in 1938 and lasted until September 1956. The lenses below the No 11 route number were for the Corporation's colour coding system, which allowed trams to be recognised from a distance at night. The 11, for example, showed red above white. In the background a similar tram heads for Princes Street, while a rebodied Daimler bus passes in front of Binns' 1935-built department store. *C. Banks collection / Colour-Rail (IR233)*

Heading along Lothian Road in 1956 bound for Tollcross on a short-working, Shrubhill standard No 160 of 1935 passes the 19th-century St John's Episcopal Church that sits at the west end of Princes Street. The tram carries the once-familiar advertisement for Weston's biscuits, the first advertisement to appear on the city's trams when the Corporation gave in to commercial forces in the early 1950s. To the right of the hand-painted advert is the distinctive red flag for Cowan-ad, the advertising contractors. *J. Copland / Photobus*

Two Princes Street-bound trams caught in traffic in Lothian Road waiting to turn on to the city's main thoroughfare in July 1955. No 112, Shrubhill-built in 1935, on the 9 service, has actually come from Colinton and is bound for Granton, despite the indicators. In front of it on the 6 (Marchmont Circle) is a late-model wooden Shrubhill standard, dating from the early 1930s. Beside them looms the Caledonian Hotel, which was built around Princes Street railway station, terminus for services to Glasgow Central and points on the West Coast main line, as well as local services. The station closed in September 1965. *C. Banks collection / Colour-Rail (IR231)*

Above: Two Corporation Leyland Tiger Cubs with Weymann bodies turn from Lothian Road into West Fountainbridge in March 1962. Lothian Road is the main southwestern corridor to Princes Street, today with additional traffic spilling from the West Approach Road, built on former railway trackbed. The 46 service linked Portobello, Edinburgh's eastern seaside resort, through the Old Town to Juniper Green, a village on the city's western boundary. The 19th-century buildings behind the buses are relatively undistinguished, but facing them, to the cameraman's left, is the art deco bulk of Lothian House. *Iain MacGregor*

Right: Tollcross was always a busy junction, with the added complication of a tram depot in a narrow side street. Corporation bus No 716 negotiates Tollcross in June 1974 among roadworks connected with a new one-way system and the introduction of the city's first bus lanes. The area behind the bus has now been significantly changed, with new commercial and residential developments, and even the 1960-built Goldberg's store has given way to new housing. The Leyland Titan PD2 is heading for the Torphin terminus of the 10 route. *Gavin Booth*

Edinburgh has been in the forefront of introducing bus-priority measures, more recently with its extensive network of Greenways. In 1974 it created the city's first bus lane, in Earl Grey Street, and Corporation Leyland PD2 No 515 on the 15 route bound for Joppa uses the newly operational facility in July 1974. The dark building above the bus is the Methodist Central Hall. Ahead of the bus on the right of the photograph is the brooding bulk of Lothian House in Lothian Road, and in front of this an Alexander-bodied Leyland PD2 turns right into Fountainbridge. *Gavin Booth*

Beyond Tollcross the road to the south leads through the pleasant open space of Bruntsfield Links, with 19th-century tenements and villas enjoying an open outlook across the city. Corporation Leyland PD2 No 566 heads for the southern edge of the city at Fairmilehead in April 1975. It carries a once-familiar advert for Bell's whisky — though the Ford D-series van carries supplies of the rival Haig brand. *Gavin Booth*

Left: A Leyland Tiger Cub, on the 1 service, makes its descent of Johnston Terrace from the Old Town towards the Tollcross area in September 1961. Photographed from the Castle Esplanade, home to August's annual Edinburgh Military Tattoo, Arthur's Seat, the city's 823ft-high extinct volcano, looms above the stone-built houses. The ridge of cliffs, Salisbury Crags, leads north towards the Palace of Holyroodhouse. The multi-chimneyed buildings to the right of the bus lead to the Grassmarket, an historic open space full of atmosphere, with the Castle as its dramatic backdrop. The 1 service was a direct descendant of the Corporation's first proper bus service, introduced in 1919, serving the Easter Road, Royal Mile and Fountainbridge areas that had never had cable or electric trams. It boasted an intensive frequency of single-deck buses until 1966,

when rebuilding of low bridges allowed the use of double-deckers. *Iain MacGregor*

Below: Passing the High Kirk of St Giles, in the High Street, is a 1966 Corporation Leyland Titan PD3 on the 1 Circle route — except it's early evening in June 1973 and the bus will not quite complete a full circle, only going as far as London Street, where it will come off service to return to Central garage. Parts of St Giles date back to the 15th and 16th centuries, while the building on the right was built in the early 20th century for Midlothian County Council, later becoming Lothian Region Chambers and now the Visitor Centre for the Scottish Parliament. *Roy Marshall / Photobus*

Left: On a City Tour in the Canongate, the eastern continuation of the High Street and part of the historic Royal Mile, a Corporation Bedford YRT with Duple coach body pauses outside the Canongate Kirk (out of sight to the right) in July 1974. On the left is the 16th-century Huntly House, now The Museum of Edinburgh, and the 19th-century clock tower on the right indicates the Canongate Tolbooth, again 16th-century, and again now a museum, in this case The People's Story, dealing with working life in the city. *Gavin Booth*

Above: In the 1960s and 1970s many of the buildings in the Royal Mile were rebuilt and restored, with varying degrees of success, including White Horse Close, on the right of the picture. This close (alley) is itself well worth seeing, but the strange 1960s arcaded front prevents many visitors from realising what is behind. The 1975 Corporation Bedford YRT coach, seen when new, pauses while the driver comments on the buildings at the foot of the Royal Mile. The new Scottish Parliament complex is presently taking shape on the opposite side of the road. *Gavin Booth*

Above: Just a short distance from the Palace of Holyroodhouse is one of the bridges that caused Edinburgh Corporation to keep a substantial fleet of single-deck buses. In 1966 the roadway under these bridges was lowered to allow double-deckers to work busy routes like the 1 Circle, and passing under one of the Abbeymount bridges carrying the East Coast main line between Waverley and King's Cross, is one of the 50 Leyland Titan PD2s bought in 1961/2. It carries an illuminated advertisement panel — a short-lived 1960s fashion, as the blank panel suggests. This bus is now one of a growing number of former Edinburgh Corporation vehicles in preservation. *Gavin Booth*

Right: Holyrood Park is Edinburgh's great open area, dominated by Arthur's Seat and fringed on all sides by the city. On a fine day in July 1975 an Eastern Scottish Bedford YRQ coach on the City Sightseeing tour passes along Queen's Drive before making its circuit of the park. The Palace of Holyroodhouse is on the right, and above that the outline of Calton Hill. The grassed area is being prepared for a Royal review of the troops. *Gavin Booth*

Left: Queen's Drive winds right round Holyrood Park and offers breathtaking views of the city. With St Margaret's Loch in the background, a 1972 Corporation Bedford YRT with Duple body on a City Tour starts on the climb in July 1975. The photographer's children wave to the tourists, possibly spontaneously. *Gavin Booth*

Right: Leaning over as it tackles the awkward camber where York Place leads into North St Andrew Street in June 1963, Corporation Leyland-bodied Titan PD2 No 253 is on the 42, one of several circular routes introduced in the 1950s. New in 1952, the bus has been modernised by the Corporation, with a glassfibre front end in place of its previous exposed radiator. Now a busy corridor into the city centre, York Place contains some fine 18th- and 19th-century buildings that often go unnoticed in the constant bustle. *A. J. Douglas / Photobus*

Right: Grinding up North St Andrew Street, linking York Place with St Andrew Square, is one of 16 wartime Daimlers that were rebodied to help with the tram-replacement programme. Seen here in June 1963, No 373 was new in 1944 and received this Alexander body in 1954, effectively disguising its age. The fact that it has a Leyland-style front end is a consequence of ECT's adoption of glassfibre and the need for standardisation. The bus survived until 1967. The weathered red sandstone building with the pinnacles is the Venetian Gothic style National Portrait Gallery. *Iain MacGregor*

Below: The main road between Edinburgh and the once independent burgh of Leith starts at the east end of Princes Street as the narrow Leith Street, then broadens out into Leith Walk, leading down to the city's port. The top of Leith Street changed during the period covered by this book, with the demolition of the St James's Square area and the construction of the new St James Centre developments. As shoppers walk up towards the new centre on the right, a Corporation Leyland Atlantean picks up and drops passengers on route 5 to the eastern suburbs at Brunstane in January 1974. ECT adopted dual-door buses in the late 1960s to deal with the many busy stops in the city centre. Above the bus is the 19th-century General Post Office, currently being developed for office use, while the dark building on the right is the uncleaned North British Hotel. *Gavin Booth*

Right: Intending passengers at the bus stop in March 1974 seem unimpressed by the Corporation Leyland Tiger Cub on the Shoppabus circle, in spite of the 4p fare. On what the Scots would describe as a 'dreich' day, No 94 is on the North Bridge bound for Princes Street. Behind it is the office of *The Scotsman* newspaper — now the five-star Scotsman Hotel. The present North Bridge, linking the High Street with Princes Street as it soars over Waverley station, is a century old. *Arnold Richardson / Photobus*

Right: Elm Row, one of the streets that form part of Leith Walk, has always been a busy point for buses, partly due to the proximity of Edinburgh Corporation's Central garage in Annandale Street. Against a background of 19th-century buildings, two Leyland Atlanteans pick up on their way towards the east end of Princes Street in June 1973. No 802 on the 49 route for Little France was new in 1966 and was one of the first two Corporation buses to have panoramic side windows on its Alexander body, a feature that would characterise new Edinburgh double-deckers for the next 15 years. When new, 802 undertook a goodwill mission to Florence, one of Edinburgh's twin cities. *Roy Marshall / Photobus*

Left: On the first part of its long journey to Fairmilehead in July 1956, tram 91 of 1937 vintage crosses the Water of Leith by the amazing Bernard Street swing bridge linking The Shore at Leith with Commercial Street. There is now a fixed bridge at this point, and the surrounding area has become very fashionable.
J. Copland / Photobus

Below left: In the last months of the tramway system, 1935 Shrubhill standard No 55 heads for Granton along Lindsay Road. Behind the tram, Commercial Street stretches back to Bernard Street and Leith's commercial heart. Behind the building on the left is Leith Docks. The building, which survives today, was still in use as Leith North railway terminus, with services from Princes Street station until August 1962. Beyond this building today are the vast Ocean Terminal shopping and leisure complex and the former Royal Yacht *Britannia*.
J. Copland / Photobus

This area was used as the Stanley Road terminus for the 7, 11 and 28 trams until 1949, when the route was extended down existing tracks on Craighall Road to Newhaven. No 353, which has climbed from Newhaven on its journey to the Braids, was built with open balconies at Shrubhill in 1926; these were enclosed five years later, and it survived until 1955. *J. Robertson / Colour-Rail*

Left: Although it was billed on the trams as Stanley Road, the terminus for the 7, 11 and 28 trams was latterly the foot of Craighall Road, a point that is more accurately described on today's buses as Newhaven, right on the Firth of Forth and in sight of the hills of Fife. The small building set into the sea wall was a toilet provided for Corporation staff. No 50, one of the last five standard cars built at Shrubhill, in 1950, sits at this terminus in 1956 before heading south again. No 50 saw barely six years' service, surviving to the closure of the tramway system in 1956. *J. Copland / Photobus*

Right: The track down Craighall Road continued east to link with the coastal tramway between Leith and Granton, but the connection was rarely used. In this 1956 view, the Craighall Road track comes in on the right, though tram 48 will continue west along the Forth shore to Granton. Over the wall on the left of the photograph is Newhaven Harbour and the fish market, the latter now, appropriately, a Harry Ramsden's restaurant. Tram 48, new in 1950, was another short-lived example, but it survived to take part in the final procession in November 1956. *J. Copland / Photobus*

Right: Granton Square, next to the harbour built in Victorian times to export coal, was a busy hub for Edinburgh Corporation tram and bus services. No fewer than five routes terminated here, and the 13/14 'circle' cars also passed through. No 265 on the 13 prepares to continue its figure-of-eight through Leith and the city centre back to Churchhill — displayed as 'Church Hill' on this car. In the background of this August 1955 view, No 157 is ready to return south to Colinton. No 265 was one of two experimental all-metal cars, built in 1933 by Metro-Cammell, which lasted until 1956. Its general similarity to what became the Shrubhill 1934 standard design is obvious. The building on the right, built in the 19th century as the Granton Inn, is HMS *Claverhouse*, used by the Royal Naval Volunteer Reserve. *I. Davidson / Colour-Rail*

Left: One of the last new trams built at Shrubhill by the Corporation, tram 48 of 1950 pauses for breath at Granton before continuing its figure-of-eight journey to upmarket Churchhill in August 1955. It offers a good opportunity to consider the classic lines of the Edinburgh standard tram. Unlike other big-city fleets, including Glasgow, Leeds and London, which operated big bogie trams, Edinburgh stuck to four-wheel trucks and built trams that were just 30ft long, with seats for just 62 passengers; Glasgow's contemporary 'Coronation' trams were 34ft long with 65 seats. While Glasgow's later trams were sleek and brash, Edinburgh's were rather more restrained. The driver's platform was open to the elements, although a door spared him draughts from the upper deck. The driver had a rudimentary 'seat', but many preferred to stand at the controls. The madder and white livery was relieved by gold and red lining-out, and the window surrounds were painted in brown, giving a wood effect. *I. Davidson / Colour-Rail (IR415)*

Left: Granton Road station was the northern terminus of the busy 23 service, one of the last two tram routes to be withdrawn, in November 1956. The station itself was below road level, on the former Caledonian Railway line linking Princes Street and Leith North stations. Tram 120 of 1936 is ready to move forward over the crossover to return to Morningside station, on the former North British Railway Suburban Circle, in July 1956. *J. Copland / Photobus*

In the 1950s Edinburgh Corporation was experimenting with simplified liveries on its buses, with a view to saving costs by spray-painting them, and this 1959 Leyland Titan PD3 with Alexander bodywork was delivered in an all-over bright red scheme with gold lining-out. Bright red had featured on the Corporation's tram livery and has more recently appeared on the 'harlequin' livery worn by Lothian Buses' low-floor vehicles. No 999 ran like this until repainted into normal madder and white in 1962. It was normally found on the 19 Circle route, and is resting at the Pilton layover point in July 1959. The local-authority housing in the Pilton area dates from the 1930s and was always served by buses. *Gavin Booth collection*

Left: In June 1975 a line of Eastern Scottish single-deckers queues up in George Square to transport delegates and their wives, in the city for a Radiology Conference, on a tour to see Hopetoun House and the Forth Bridges. Eastern Scottish was often required to provide large numbers of vehicles for conferences like this. All of the vehicles have Alexander Y-type bodies, built in Falkirk, and the leading coach is a 1973 Bedford YRQ. George Square was one of the city's 18th-century gems but was controversially 'developed' in the 20th century, and only the west side is still original. Edinburgh University occupies much of the area, and the buildings on the

north side, behind the buses, demonstrate the architectural mixture that can now be found. *Gavin Booth*

Above: Eastern Scottish and its predecessors operated an intensive network of bus services to the Midlothian coalfield, to the south of the city. This 1971 Daimler Fleetline with Eastern Coach Works body heads for the mining village of Rosewell in March 1973, passing Playfair's 19th-century Surgeon's Hall in Nicolson Street. *Iain MacGregor*

Below: Beyond the busy shopping area around Salisbury, the road to the south opens out towards Newington, and in March 1967 Guy Arab IV No 922 takes advantage of its freedom as it speeds down Minto Street, passing sedate early-19th-century villas. There were 70 of these Guys bought to help complete the tram replacement in the mid-1950s, yet, while examples of most notable postwar classes of Edinburgh Corporation bus are represented in preservation, none of these Guys survives. Unless, of course, anyone knows otherwise . . . *Iain MacGregor*

Right: Liberton was the most southerly point reached by trams on the Bridges routes. Two routes terminated here — the 1 and the 7. In the 1930s approval had been granted for an extension of the tramway to Kaimes, but this was abandoned. Tram 231 on the 7 awaits its time to return to Stanley Road in July 1955; the 7 was replaced by buses in March the following year. Tram 231 is of interest: although at first glance very similar to a Shrubhill-built standard, it is in fact one of three all-metal cars built in 1934 by Hurst Nelson of Motherwell, which lasted in the fleet until 1956. This one uniquely carried advertising for Edinburgh Zoo.
C. Banks collection / Colour-Rail

Right: Fairmilehead was the most southerly terminus of the Edinburgh tramway system, although, had prewar plans come to fruition, it would have been extended to Hillend. At the terminus in July 1956, ready to make its long run to Stanley Road, on the Firth of Forth, is tram No 214 on the 11 service. The tramway had been gradually extended on this corridor during the 1930s to cater for new housing, and had only reached Fairmilehead in 1936. Tram 214 was one of just eight built at Shrubhill during World War 2; it was withdrawn in 1956. *J. Copland / Photobus*

Below right: A 1955 Fairmilehead view shows the shape of things to come. The conductor, complete with white-topped cap, has just reversed the trolley as tram 202 prepares to return to Stanley Road in July 1955. On the right is a recently delivered Leyland Titan PD2 on the 15 service, which had replaced the tram service in September 1954. The 11 tram would be withdrawn in September 1956, one of the last four routes to survive. Tram 202 survived right to the end of the system. *C. Banks collection / Colour-Rail*

Far right: Looking rather sorry for itself, travel-stained 1931 standard No 264 sits at the Craigentinny Avenue terminus on a dull July day in 1955 as the driver sets the front destination for its return to Tollcross. The tram survived only until the end of the year, but the 19 route lasted until May 1956. Beyond the wall beside the tram is the railway to Leith Docks, and beyond that the Firth of Forth. Today, on reclaimed land beyond what remains of the railway, is the city's sewage-treatment works, the sometimes pungent presence of which may mean that an ice-cream seller has less chance of doing business today than did his predecessor more than 45 years ago. *C. Banks collection / Colour-Rail (IR234)*

Left: Climbing from Meadowbank to Abbeyhill on the 26 — always one of the Corporation's core services — recently delivered Leyland Atlantean No 426 was photographed in March 1975. These buses were among the last delivered to Edinburgh Corporation Transport Department before regionalisation in May 1975. The building on the left has been converted into flats, as with so many of the city's older properties. *Gavin Booth*

Below left: Built for the 1970 Commonwealth Games, Meadowbank Stadium is on the A1 road east of the city centre, and bordering the main East Coast railway line. Passing the stadium in March 1975 is a well-filled 1970 Corporation Atlantean on the 44 route linking Eastfield, on the city's eastern boundary, with Juniper Green, on the west. Following deregulation in 1986, the 44 was one of the services that was extended beyond both boundaries to serve new areas. *Gavin Booth*

Right: Rattling over the cobbles in Brighton Place, Portobello, in 1974 is a 10-year-old Leyland Titan PD3 on the 12 service to Hay Drive, Niddrie — an extension of the former 12 tram route to the south. The bus is about to pass under the East Coast railway line and the site of the former Portobello station. The late-19th-century villas in Brighton Place owe their existence to the coming of the railway in the middle of that century. Although it appears to be a fine day, the front doors of the bus should not be open. The 'broadside' style of advertisement, here for a local staff agency, was a 1970s fashion. *Gavin Booth*

Above: Edinburgh used to be surrounded by reminders of its industrial past. Here at Niddrie in 1976 are remnants of the former brickworks and the industrial railways of the area as a 1960 Leyland Tiger Cub crosses the path of an abandoned level crossing. This area has since been totally transformed with the building of the Fort Kinnaird shopping and leisure complex. *Gavin Booth*

Right: One of the 'streamliners' sits at the King's Road, Portobello, terminus in May 1954. These were supplied in 1934/5 by outside contractors; No 14 was built in 1935 by Hurst Nelson at Motherwell and survived with ECT until the summer of 1956. It is ready to return to Corstorphine on the 12 route, which was withdrawn in June 1954. King's Road was where the tramway from Leith linked with the main tramway from the city centre, and was the site of a large power station. Today the power station has given way to housing, and beyond the pub on the left of the photograph is now Lothian Buses' Marine garage. *D. A. Kelso / Colour-Rail (IR508)*

Well to the east of Edinburgh — so far east, in fact, that it's at the east end of Musselburgh — tram 120 waits at the Levenhall terminus of service 21 until the previous tram has cleared the single track there. The 21 tram started in 1923 after the last cable cars in Edinburgh ran to the Joppa terminus, when it became possible to run electric cars through from Edinburgh to Musselburgh. From 1923 there was also a 22 tram that ran all the way to Port Seton, but the 21 was extended to Levenhall when the section beyond that point was abandoned in 1928. The last 21 trams ran in November 1954, and the replacement buses stayed within the Edinburgh boundary at Eastfield. The fencing behind the tram is the edge of Musselburgh Racecourse. The red box on the tram's platform is an honesty box for uncollected fares. Tram 120 was built at Shrubhill in 1936 and gave 20 years' service. *J. Robertson / Colour-Rail*

The select Ravelston Dykes area, nestling between the Corstorphine and Queensferry roads, has never required a high level of bus service, and in the 1970s the Corporation experimented with hail- and-ride services in some of the quieter roads in the area, picking up where required. This 1973 Seddon Midi 25-seater is seen in October 1974. *Gavin Booth*

Left: Leafy Colinton, on the southwest of the city, was terminus for the 9 and 10 trams, both of which started their journeys at different points on the Forth coastline. In August 1955 No 193 has arrived at Colinton; though its blind is already set for the return journey to Granton, it has yet to move forward over the crossover on to the other track. No 193 was a Shrubhill wooden standard and lasted until October 1955, the month the 9 and 10 routes were converted to bus operation.
The SMT Guy Arab double-decker in the background is heading through Colinton for Balerno, which at the time was beyond the city boundary.
I. Davidson / Colour-Rail (IR416)

Right: From the 1920s Edinburgh expanded along the Calder Road to the west with housing and industrial developments.
The tramway system reached only as far west as Stenhouse on this corridor, and bus services provided transport to Sighthill, which marked the city boundary.
The 34/35 services got to Sighthill by convoluted routes that largely avoided Princes Street, and No 600, new in 1956 and the last of the second 100 tram-replacement Leyland Titan PD2s, is seen negotiating one of several Calder Road roundabouts in October 1973.
Gavin Booth

Front cover: Edinburgh's trams were a popular and integral part of city life until the mid-1950s, when buses took over, and this July 1954 view at the west end of Princes Street shows two of the most familiar types of tram waiting on Lothian Road, ready to turn eastwards on to Princes Street. No 253 was built to the Edinburgh Corporation design by Pickering in 1933, and its companion is a prewar standard car, built by Edinburgh Corporation at its Shrubhill Works. Recently delivered Leyland Titan buses on the Corstorphine services are seen in the background. The huge Binns department store dates from the same decade as the trams. Forming the western end of the Princes Street shops, this was (and still is) a popular city-centre meeting point, and, although the store now carries the 'Frasers' name, many older people still make arrangements to meet at 'Binns corner'. *Colour-Rail*

Back cover: An Edinburgh Corporation Leyland Titan PD2 heads assorted newer Corporation Leylands (an Atlantean on the 33 and a Tiger Cub on the circular Shoppabus route) westwards along Princes Street. ECT bought 300 of these Titans with ultra-lightweight Metro-Cammell Orion bodies for tram replacement, and an Edinburgh bailie aired his views on them at the time saying: 'They are ungainly, inelegant, monstrous masses of shivering tin. They are modern to the extent of being able to produce a perfect synchronisation of rock 'n' roll'. The phrase 'monstrous masses of shivering tin' has passed into bus folklore. No 500, seen here heading for the Torphin terminus of the 9 route, was the last bus of the first batch of 100 Titans. *Gavin Booth*

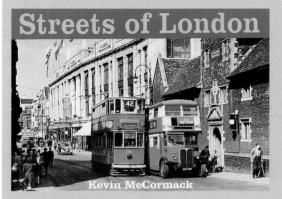